Advance
Prep
Trai
Security Officers

Emergency Preparedness training; written for the Security Officer, working in the field, to prepare them to take action, when an emergencies arises.

The Mission of this training series; is to bring about an awareness, of the important role, a Professional Security Officer plays, in the protection of the Nations assets and encourage the training of Private Security Officers to attain a Professional image.

Security Officer Training Series
Author Charles E. Neuf CPP
Training Police, Private
Investigators and Security

First Printing July 2002
Revised Second Printing January
2009
Revised Third Printing January 2011

No part of this booklet may be used
without written permission of the
Author Charles E. Neuf CPP
Copyright 2011

ISBN 978-1-257-09548-3

9 781257 095483   90000

Security is as old as time itself. Security came into existence before Police.

Ezekiel 33:6 (Old Testament)
"If a watchman sees the sword coming and does not blow the trumpet to warn the people and the sword comes and takes the life of one of them." "I will hold the watchman accountable for his Blood."

The Security Officer, in most instances; is the first line of defense to give the alarm when something is wrong on their post.

The responsibility of training; lies with the person who represents themselves, as qualified to be a Security Officer and their employer who represents to a client, they will provide trained and experienced Security Officers, for the clients protection.

Introduction

Emergency Preparedness of Private Security Officers is vital in protecting the assets of a private business. Even before September 11, 2001, it was known that private businesses would be the targets of terrorists.

The Emergency Preparedness training series for Private Security Officers has been developed by Charles E. Neuf CPP, a Security Consultant, and Business Contingency Planner of over 30 years, to prepare the Private Security Officer to handle emergencies and protect the assets of their client.

This Emergency Preparedness training series was designed to provide the Private Security Officer with instruction, on how to handle an emergency, while on post, in a professional manner.

The training series consists of, "Basic's of Emergency Preparedness" and "Advanced Training for Emergency Preparedness.

Certificate of attendance / Certificate of Completion

Security Officers who attend Emergency Preparedness training will receive a Certificate of Attendance and those attending both the basic and advanced courses of the series will receive a Certificate of Completion as an "Emergency Preparedness Trained" Security Professional.

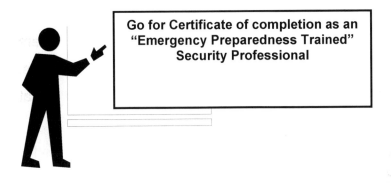

Go for Certificate of completion as an "Emergency Preparedness Trained" Security Professional

Advanced Emergency Preparedness Training

A Security Training Series

Emergency Preparedness training; is written for the

Security Officer working in the field, Preparing them to take an action, when emergencies occurs.

Charles E. Neuf CPP, *"The Major"*
Security Training Solutions

Charles E Neuf CPP is the author of the Security Training Solutions series, for Private Security. The Major has been involved in training police and private Security for more than 30 years.

The Mission of this training series; is to bring about an awareness, of the important role, a Professional Security Officer plays, in the protection of the Nations assets and encourage the training of Private Security Officers to attain a Professional image.

Contents

- o Follow emergency procedures
- o Giving directions
- o Staying on the phone

Chapter four

- Working with Emergency Services;
  - o Who is in-charge?
  - o Knowing your Post
  - o Notification by priority

Chapter five

- Reporting the details of an Emergency;
  - o Make notes first
  - o Writing the report
  - o Reporting details

Chapter six

- What can happen after the emergency
  - o What Security Officer needs to do
  - o Insurance claims
  - o Who's at fault
  - o Just the facts "Ma'am"

**Security
Officers
Protecting
The
Assets
Of
American
Businesses
24/7**

How this training course will be
Presented, "Talking with the Major"

The writing style of the author; is that of a friend and mentor. Envision yourself seated at a table with a cup of coffee or a soda, talking with the Major about an incident that occurred on your post.

Your having a discussion about "how to" handle this occurrence and your friend the Major, is relating to you his experiences, from his 40 years of handling Police and Security matters.

The Major wants to help you solve some of the perplexing problems a Security Officer faces. He is being honest with you, by relating things he knows can happen. The Major knows that not all problems have the same set of circumstances; therefore, circumstances sometimes change the action to take.

He knows no one can give you an action, to take for everything that happens, therefore; the action you take is based on your decision. What the Major wants to do is share his experiences and knowledge with you, so you will have something to base your actions on.

The Writing Plan; what you can expect as a format for this writing.

The Mission; each chapter will start with a mission of what we want to accomplish, in the chapter.

Then, what we will talk about; what we will talk about in the chapter.

A Scenario; a scenario is a story; a story or reference about the subject that you can relate to.

Details; this will be about the subject and some things you can do.

This writing plan, will give you an understanding, of what we will be covering in each chapter; it also keeps The Major on track when he is writing.

"I love it when a plan comes to-gather"; do you know what TV Series that quote came from? (The "A Team")

A self-test *Testing is your way of determining how you are doing in the understanding* department.

The test answers will be provided for some questions in your training booklet and others can only be answered by you. Self-testing allows one to judge themselves.

Chapter One

People First in
Emergencies

- *Know when to Evacuate*

- *Know the Evacuation
  Plan*

- *OSHA Requirements*

This chapter's mission

Stressing the Safety of People, is always, the number one priority in the evacuation of an area, and to provide the Security Officer with an explanation, on using an evacuation plan.

What we will be talking about

In an emergency people always, come first. Having an evacuation plan and following that plan assures safety of people in an evacuation. OSHA is a federal agency that protects the worker in many safety areas; the evacuation plan is one of those areas required by businesses for their workers.

- **Check to see if your post has an evacuation plan as soon as you are assigned, and review the plan.**

Scenario; making an evacuation, without knowing, what the evacuation procedures are;

The fire alarm sounds, the Security Officer is contacted and told to have everyone evacuate the building. What will the Security Officer do?

The officer knows the safety of people, is the first thing to take care of, and they begin to tell all persons to leave the building. Those being told to leave ask questions.

- What is happening?
- What door should I leave by?
- When can I get back in the building?
- Can I go back to my office to shut down the computer?
- I am not leaving unless this is a real emergency, is it?
- Where do I go until I can get back in the building?
- Has the Fire Department been called?

Can a Security Officer handle this evacuation in a professional way; if the Officer had never been trained on what to do at this location and they are not aware of the any emergency evacuation plan?

An evacuation plan would answer all of these questions for the security officer before the event takes place.

The Building Evacuation

A building evacuation is a serious thing. What about all the people who cannot walk down 10 or 15 flights of stairs? Some may be in wheel chairs; others may not have good balance and could fall. Injuries can occur in an evacuation and cause confusion and panic.

Evacuation plans

Most businesses locations are required to have an evacuation plan. OSHA requires an evacuation plan in writing and the plan to be explained to all employees' and all new employees'.

Most cities have requirements for all multi-floor building to have a fire plan and all persons working or living in the building must have the plan explained to them and hold regular fire alarm drills.

Evacuation Plan Testing

All businesses and buildings requiring an evacuation plan are also required to test the plan at regular intervals. Some cities will send someone out from the fire department to observe the test.

Security Officers on location need to know about and be tested on the evacuation plan.

In most instances, the Security Officer on duty will be looked at as the person in-charge of the evacuation. The evacuation plan explains how the building evacuation will be conducted and who, what, when, where why and how of the evacuation.

In a multi-floor building, all the elevators go to the ground floor and the doors open and stay open until the firefighters clear the alarm.

There is a special elevator key at each location, for emergency responders to release the elevator for use. Find out about the key location on your post, before your ask for it.

Question the security officer must know the answer to;

- **Who is in charge of the evacuation**
  Someone must be responsible for what is taking place.
- **Who will give the order to evacuation**
  Who gives the order to evacuate?
- **What will happen**

What will happen, alarms will sound, elevators will shut down, lights will go on in the stairs area, etc.

- **When to evacuate**

  What is needed to start an evacuation?

- **Where everyone will go after evacuation**

  People need to know where to go.

- **How the evacuation will be conducted**

  Orderly, a floor at a time, quickly or slowly, how will it be done?

- **Why there will be an evacuation**

  Knowing why there is an evacuation will determine how it will be done.

People first rule.

Remember, safety of people is the first consideration in an evacuation. The whole reason for the evacuation plan is to keep anyone from being injured or left behind.

 **The**

People

First

Rule

Test Time

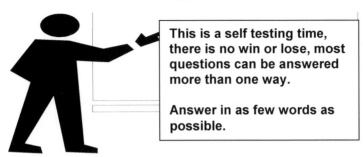

This is a self testing time, there is no win or lose, most questions can be answered more than one way.

Answer in as few words as possible.

There will be a question from each chapter we have covered to this point, answer the question and then check the chapter to see if you are on track.

One, what are the three phases of an emergency?

Two, how can one keep a crisis from turning into an emergency?

Three, when an emergency is involved, describe what it means when the Security Officer reacts to a condition.

Four, what is the difference between post orders and company policy & procedure?

Five, what is an evacuation plan?

Chapter Two

What are the most common Emergencies Security Officers are faced with?

 **Fire**

And

Water

Accidents and Injuries

- Most Common Emergencies

- Preventive Measures

- Handling the Emergency

This chapter's mission

To prepare the Security Officer to handle the most common Emergencies they may encounter, in a professional manner.

What we will be talking about

Damages and dangers involved in emergencies, most commonly encounter by the Security Officer. These are Fire, Water, Personal injuries, and illness. Preventive measures, as well as handling the emergency.

Scenario one, the fire alarm sounds.

Suggested action, Determine as quickly as possible if there is a fire or is it an alarm problem.

How do you do this, it depends on the location.
- Check the alarm panel, if there is one
- Check the area of the alarm, if you can
- Radio or telephone other areas at the location
- Telephone the alarm company and ask for the location of the alarm sounding.

Scenario two, it is a fire! Notify the fire department with details.

Suggested action, Get the person responsible to issue an evacuation order. If the Security Officer is responsible for evacuation, they follow the evacuation plan instructions.

How do you do this, again it depends on the location.

- Are other persons on location to order evacuation
- Are there evacuation instructions available
- Is the alarm system setup to automatically call the Fire Department?

Scenario three, The sprinkler system begins to activate and water is flowing into the building and onto everything.

About this scenario and sprinkler systems

Sprinkler systems come in various configurations and most are under lock and key security. Not only are most in a locked room, but the valves them selves are under chain and lock.

If the Security Officer is not trained in handling this scenario, notifying the maintenance department and your supervisor would be the best thing to do.

Preventive measures for fire alarms and sprinkler systems

- Any water leak at a sprinkler head is an emergency
  - o Notify maintenance and your supervisor

- If there is no training provided for fire emergencies ask for it. Find out where the evacuation plan is and read it

- Any time a smoke alarm gives off sounds of some kind, even a chirp, report it in writing and follow-up for repair.

Scenario four, there is a person who is injured or becomes ill on your post.

Suggested action, first give aid by finding out what the medical problem is and comfort the person involved, by reassuring them help is on the way.

At this point, much depends on the first aid training the Security Officer has.

- If the Officer is trained in first aid, then immediate provide first aid to prevent further progression of what is happening

- Someone should be sent to telephone for emergency services.

- If the Security Officer is not trained in first aid get someone to stay with the injured / Ill, and escort emergency services personnel to the scene.

Test Time

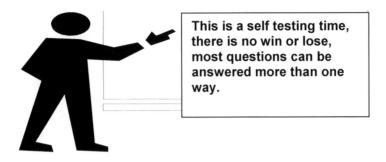

This is a self testing time, there is no win or lose, most questions can be answered more than one way.

What are the most common emergencies that may be encountered on your post?

_____

_____What happens when a fire alarm sounds in a building that has elevators?

_____

_____Have you ever read an evacuation plan for your post?   YES------NO-----

On your post, what would you do if an fire alarm sounded?_____

_____

<u>Chapter Three</u>

 Contacting
Emergency
Services

About making calls for Emergency
Services

When do you call 911?

Information needed for Emergency
Services calls

Emergency calls to Fire, Police and
Medical Emergency Services

The mission for this chapter; to provide a guide lines for the Security Officer, to use in calling for Emergency Services to assist, in an emergency, on their post.

What we will be talking about

What to do and how to summons emergency Services in an emergency.

Real Life scenarios

If you were to call for Police and did not tell the dispatcher an armed man was in your building, the Officer responding could be killed, all due to the lack of information.

When Fire and Medical calls are made, time is important, detailed information is needed to get the right equipment needed, to the right location.

If something has happened inside your building, and access is by the rear door only, and the emergency vehicles come to the front door, valuable time will be lost.

About making Emergency Calls

Emergency Services are important part of the business community. Emergency Services Personnel are required to meet training standards for their profession.

Specialized equipment is available to be used for special emergencies, and time can be saved if the equipment needed is known in the beginning.

When telephoning Police, Fire, Rescue, or Medical emergency services, they need to know what they will be faced with and the type of equipment needed to meet your emergency.

Information you supply can assist responders in determining the number of units and the type of equipment needed.

Not supplying enough information may, put emergency personnel in "Harms way" or may cause the loss of life, because specialized equipment is not available.

When do you call 911?

When there is a "**real emergency**" requiring immediate action to prevent injury, loss of life or destruction of property.

What is a "real emergency"?

- Serious injury, life threatening
- Harm will come to someone, if Police do not arrive quickly.
- Fire

- Physical threats made to someone

What is considered, "Not an emergency"

- Minor injury, no threat to life
- You want to report something such as an auto accident, something missing or need information.

Real life scenario

- A heart attack calls for a Paramedic, call 911.
- A fall or minor injury may call for Ambulance transportation, but it is not always an emergency.

First; consider the equipment needed, there are only a few Paramedic units available; if you tie up one of these units and a "real emergency" occurs, the unit will not be available to respond.

Second, consider the cost. Local ambulance companies often provide non-emergency transportation for half the cost of a Paramedic equipped unit.

Most emergency calls are taken by dispatchers who are trained, to work with emergencies, they will ask questions and try to get as much information as possible, before dispatching an emergency unit.

Be prepared to provide emergency information needed by asking questions of those involved before making the call. Follow the format for making emergency telephone calls.

EMPLOYEE EVACUATION PROCEDURES; when a building Fire alarm sounds; all Employees should begin Emergency Shutdown Procedures.

The Supervisor In-Charge of the Evacuation will be responsible for making a quick check on why the alarm is sounding and will give the evacuation order if needed.

Should an employee feel threatened by the alarm, they should evacuate the building without the Supervisors order to evacuate, and proceed to the assembly area and await instructions.

EVACUATION PROCEDURES

1. Remain calm

2. Begin emergency equipment shutdown and record removal.

3. Await the supervisor's report and evacuation instructions.

4. Take your keys and personal items with you.

5. Follow the evacuation plan procedures.

6. Use the evacuation route established.

7. Assist disabled persons

8. The last person out should close doors, but do not lock them.

9. The Supervisor for their area will make a final building inspection.

10. Go directly to the Evacuation Assembly area.

11. Report to the person in-charge and be sure your name is listed as being at the assembly area.

12. Do not leave the assembly area until advised to do so.

13. Do not re-enter building until directed to do so by emergency personnel.

TELEPHONING POLICE

When receiving a request to call Police _ALWAYS_ obtain the following information, _BEFORE MAKING THE CALL!_

1. Who wants the police called
   a. Get full name and whom they represent.

2. Why the Police are wanted, the reason.

3. Is this an Emergency? Why
   a. Where do they need to go?

4. If in doubt call management for location.

5. If you call Police, notify management ASAP.

Non-Emergency phone number

Police_____

Emergency Number 911

Advise Police

1. Your name
2. Your company
3. State why your calling
4. Reason you need Police
5. Location Police should go to
6. Your phone number

CONFIRM POLICE ARE BEING SENT, ASK,

"Is the Officer being dispatched now?"

<u>***Contact the person requesting the police;***</u>

1. Advise them Police have been dispatched.

2. Have the party who requested the police to wait at the location the Police were sent to.

3. Contact Management or Security and have them go to the location where the Police will be.

4. Management or Security should obtain details of what happened and submit a report.

Each emergency call received is dispatched to an Officer in the field. The Officer must have enough information to determine how they will respond to the call.

FYI, Emergency Services 911, receives hundreds of calls each day, the dispatcher will ask you for information, be prepared to answer questions.

Alarm Sounds

There is no sign of Smoke or Fire

This is a Non-Emergency

1. **Do not silence the Alarm**

2. **Do not reset the Alarm**

3. **Contact Management**

4. **Advise Management, *Area the alarm is in.* *You have not reset alarm.***

In many Cities, it is a violation to reset a Fire Alarm in a commercial building. Only the Fire Dept. or Alarm Company should do this.

Contact the Fire Dept.
Non-Emergency
Phone

_____

Give the Fire Department the following information:

- Your name
- Your Company name
- Address of the building involved
- There is a Fire Alarm at your location:

There is no Smoke or Fire

Management is checking the building and will have a status report in 5 minutes.

OR

If you know the status, give the reason for the alarm.

Ask the fire Dept.

"What do you want us to do?"

- Do you want us to evacuate the building?

- Do you want us to wait for someone from the Fire Department to check the building?

Relate to management what the Fire Dept. wants done.

Emergency Fire Procedure

EMERGENCY

FIRE DEPT. NEEDED

TELEPHONE # 911

Advise the Dispatcher:

- **Your name**

- **Your Company name**

- **There is an Emergency and Fireman is needed.**

- Tell them what is happening

- Give the Address where needed
- Tell them someone will be there to direct them where they are needed

- Obtain the assistance of a second person at the phone---Now

- Have someone go to the entrance area to meet the Fire Truck and direct them to the area needed

- Notify Management, Fire Dept. is dispatched

- Management should be handling all telephone communications

__DO NOT MAKE ANY COMMENTS__
__OR__
__RELEASE ANY INFORMATION__

A Crisis management team should meet now and begin assessing the damage and recovery steps to take.

MEDICAL EMERGENCIES

1. **When receiving a request for Medical Assistance, obtain the following information.**

Is this an emergency of life & death? Why
Who is making the request for assistance?

What is the Medical problem?

Where is the Medical assist needed?
 Directions & Details needed

Is anyone with the person needing assistance?

2. Repeat the information you have been given.

3. Assure the person assistance is being summonsed.

Call Now! # 911 Emergencies

Non-Emergency, Non-Life threatening
Medical Transportation (Ambulance)

Call #_____
When calling for Medical services

Life & Death emergency, give the following information:

We have a Medical Emergency!

What the Emergency is, describe

Address where help is needed

Give directions

Advise if someone is there to assist

Your name, Your Company name

CONTACT MANAGEMENT WITH DETAILS, ASAP

Have someone outside the building to direct the Emergency Services to the location they are needed.

EMERGENCY

MANAGEMENT CALL LIST

These numbers are confidential

Do not release these numbers

Call in order listed,
Stop calling when one is contacted.

Name_____

Home_____

Cellular_____

Pager_____

Name_____

Home_____

Cellular_____

Pager_____

 **Notes:** The Security Officers Notebook is their most important tool.

The Security Officers notebook should have dated entries and when filled stored for at least one year

Chapter Four

Working with Emergency Services

Whose in-charge?

    Knowing your post.

        Notification by priority

Mission for this chapter

To define who will be in-charge when emergency services are called for assistance. To bring to the Security Officers attention, the need to know the location of in-coming services for gas, electric and water. Instructions; for security in prioritizing notification, of management, when there is an emergency response requested.

What we will talk about

The focus of this chapter will be the subjects listed in the mission statement.

Real Life Scenario

A hospital had the smell of gas and maintenance was not able to shut off the gas. Doors in the hospital were closed in an effort to keep the smell out, finally evacuation of patients started.

The Gas Company was called and a crew came out with diagrams of where the gas shut-off was, but the Gas company crew could not find the shut-off.

The Fire Department sent fire crews to the hospital to help locate the gas supply, while the Hospital was being evacuated.

To shorten the story, the street had been widened the year before, the gas supply to the hospital had been relocated, and the Gas Company failed to make note of the relocation.

The maintenance personnel of the hospital never knew about the relocation of the shut off valves.

The lesson in this story; points to knowing where the services supply enters the building, when responders need someone to direct them to the services location.

After all, it is your building

If a water leak occurs and the basement area is flooding, you will need to direct Emergency Services to electrical services in coming line for shut off.

Back to the scenario in chapter one; the on call maintenance person cannot be located, and your supervisor did not respond. The Security Officer on duty is the first line of defense.

Who is in-charge anyway?

When Police, Fire or Ambulance services are called for help, you have invited them in because you needed help. This puts the Services you called in-charge.

If it were a Fire, the Fire Department would be in-charge, in a Police matter, the

Police would be in-charge, and when Medical aid is there, they are in-charge.

The Security Officer will be support for the Emergency Services, there will be places they need to go to and things they need to know.

Notification by priority

When things go wrong there are people who want to know what is happening, they may even want to be at the location to find out first hand.

The Security Officer should have a list of persons to contact by priority of importance. The Security Officers Notebook is the place for these numbers to be.

Notes

 **The personal notebook of the Security Officer is the property of the Security Officer.**

Chapter Four

Reporting the details
of An Emergency

- Make notes first
- Writing the report
- Report the details

The mission for this chapter

To assist the Security Officer in developing a format to follow for writing the final report for an emergency event, after the excitement and emotion of the emergency is over.

What we will talk about

The focus will be on making notes in the Officers personal notebook of the sequence of events and order of how they occurred. Formatting and writing a final report to include details.

Scenario

A person slips and falls while on the property of your client, there was a lot of activity taking place in a short time.

- A person reported to management; a person lying down in the driveway.

- The management told the security Officer to go to the driveway and check the report out.

- On leaving the building the Officer saw a man lying on his side in the parking lot area

- The Security Officer reported what he saw by radio to the property manager and an ambulance was called to the parking lot

- While waiting on the ambulance; the person told the Security Officer they were attacked by another man, who knocked them down. The victim said he thought the man that attacked him, also fell and hurt himself.

- The Security Officer stayed with the victim, until he was removed by ambulance. The EMT from the ambulance company stated the victim had a compound fracture.

The Security Officers report

I received a call to go to the parking lot where there was a man lying on the ground. He said he thought his leg was broken, I called Carol on the radio, and she called the ambulance. The ambulance attendant said he thought the man had a broken leg.

I had asked the man what happened and he said he got in a fight with another person, he fell and the other guy ran away.

This report is not acceptable, it needs more detail

- What is the injured person's name, address, phone number, age, dress and why was he on the property.

- Where was his automobile, make, year, model and color.

Here is the twist

The Police Officer came by the location about an hour after the man was removed from the parking lot and told the Property Manager;

- A man came in and reported he was knocked to the ground in the driveway at the street entrance, by an attacker who stole his brief case and ran into the parking lot and around the side of the building.

- The person told the Police he lay in the drive stunted and a person came by and said they would get Security, but they never came.
- The man's car was parked on the street and he drove himself to the Police Station to report the theft.

Chapter Five

What Happens after the emergency?

- **What the Security Officer needs to do**
- **About Insurance claims**
- **Who's at fault**
- **Just the facts "Ma'am"**

Mission;

What the Security Officer needs to do.

What we will be taking about; getting information and making reports.

Scenario; The man lying in driveway.

The Security Officer begins by asking questions and making observations.

- Start with making rough notes in your notebook

- Get things in the order as they occurred

- Date and Time, of the series of events taking place

- Exact location

- Full name, address and phone of those involved

- Get the full picture of what is happening

- Ask questions and get your information right

- "Quote" what is said, exactly to the word

- Call in the Police when acts of violence are involved

- Give thought to what is said and what you see to support or disprove the statements

- Don't let someone pressure you on the time it takes to write your report

- If the report is not neat, accurate and complete do not submit it, re-write it

- Look at the finished report as if you were receiving it from someone else, does it look good?

-

About Insurance Claims

The Security Officer should not have any responsibility concerning insurance claim, but there will be Insurance Claims Investigators wanting to see you. Do not talk with the Insurance Investigator with out your Security Supervisor.

There is no such thing as "off the record" statements, everything you say will be reported by the Insurance Investigator.

Who is at fault and just the facts "Ma'am"

The Security Office reports only the facts as they witness them or have them given to them by a witness.

No opinions, please.

Your notebook speaks for your final report, do not write it down or say something that you cannot backup with your notes. Do not allow anyone to make copies of your notes; you may have to refer to them if you go to court.

Take your time to write your final report, do not allow someone to push you into a fast final report and do not allow anyone to change your wording or put something you have no knowledge of into the report.

Get a copy of your final report and keep it in a safe place.

Background of Charles E. Neuf CPP

Writer, Publisher and Trainer on subjects of Investigation Training Police, Private Investigators, and Security since 1960

Charles Neuf served 16 years as an Illinois state trooper assigned to the state police training Academy as an instructor, state police detective, agent National Law Enforcement Intelligence Unit and member of the governor's executive protection program.

After leaving the Illinois State Police, Neuf was the CEO of one of the largest independent investigation agencies in the Midwest, providing services for major law firms and corporations.

Neuf has provided executive protection for foreign dignitaries, corporate executives and presidential candidates for more than 30 years.

Since 1990, Charles Neuf has been known in the Security world, as the "major" through assignments with various security organization as a trainer and contingency planner.

Professional organizations; (past and present).
American Society of Industrial Security
American Society of Security Educators and Trainers
National Association of legal Investigator's
International Association of Chiefs of Police,
 International Association of Narcotics Officer
www.charlesneufcpp.com   www.censupportservices.info
www.investigatorshortstories.info

Feel free to contact the Major with questions or comments, Good & Bad. Available by e-mail @

neufcharles@yahoo.com

You can find more books @ WWW. LuLu/spotlight/neufcharlesatyahoodotcom

Security is as old as time itself. Security came into existence before Police.

Ezekiel 33:6 (Old Testament) "If a watchman sees the sword coming and does not blow the trumpet to warn the people and the sword comes and takes the life of one of them." "I will hold the watchman accountable for his Blood."

The Security Officer, in most instances; is the first line of defense to give the alarm when something is wrong on their post.

The responsibility of training; lies with the person who represents themselves, as qualified to be a Security Officer and their employer who represents to a client, they will provide trained and experienced Security Officers, for the clients protection.

Advanced Emergency Preparedness Training for Security Officers

Emergency Preparedness training; written for the Security Officer, working in the field, to prepare them to take action, when an emergencies arises.

The Mission of this training series; is to bring about an awareness, of the important role, a Professional Security Officer plays, in the protection of the Nations assets and encourage the training of Private Security Officers to attain a Professional image.

Security Officer Training Series
Author Charles E. Neuf CPP

Training Police, Private Investigators
and Security

Made in United States
Orlando, FL
18 February 2024